THE PRECIOUS
BLOOD OF JESUS

THE PRECIOUS BLOOD OF JESUS

More Than Enough

By Dr. Kevin Zadai

Unless otherwise indicated, Scripture quotations are taken from the New King James Version. Copyright © 1982 by Thomas Nelson, Inc. Used by permission.

Scripture quotations marked (NLT) are taken from the Holy Bible, New Living Translation, copyright ©1996, 2004, 2015 by Tyndale House Foundation. Used by permission of Tyndale House Publishers, a Division of Tyndale House Ministries, Carol Stream, Illinois 60188. All rights reserved.

Scripture quotations marked (TPT) are from The Passion Translation®. Copyright © 2017, 2018 by Passion & Fire Ministries, Inc. Used by permission. All rights reserved. www.thePassionTranslation.com.

Scripture quotations marked (ESV) are from the ESV® Bible (The Holy Bible, English Standard Version®), copyright © 2001 by Crossway, a publishing ministry of Good News Publishers. Used by permission. All rights reserved.

Please note that Warrior Notes publishing style capitalizes certain pronouns in Scripture that refer to the Father, Son, and Holy Spirit, which may differ from some publishers' styles. Take note that the name "satan" and related names are not capitalized. We choose not to acknowledge him, even to the point of violating accepted grammatical rules. All emphasis within Scripture quotations is the author's own.

Warrior Notes Publishing
P O Box 1288
Destrehan, LA 70047

Cover design: Virtually Possible Designs

For more information about our school, go to www.warriornotesschool.com. Reach us on the internet: www.Kevinzadai.com

ISBN 13 TP: 978-1-6631-0031-3

DEDICATION

I dedicate this book to the Lord Jesus Christ. When I died during surgery and met with Jesus on the other side, He insisted that I return to life on earth and that I help people with their destinies. Because of Jesus's love and concern for people, the Lord has actually chosen to send a person back from death to help everyone who will receive that help so that their destiny and purpose are secure in Him.

I want You, Lord, to know that when You come to take me to be with You someday, it is my sincere hope that people remember not me but the revelation of Jesus Christ that You have revealed through me. I want others to know that I am merely being obedient to Your heavenly calling and mission, which is to reveal Your plan for the fulfillment of the divine destiny for each of God's children.

ACKNOWLEDGMENTS

In addition to sharing my story with everyone through the book *Heavenly Visitation: A Guide to the Supernatural,* God has commissioned me to write over fifty books and study guides. Most recently, the Lord gave me the commission to produce this book, *The Precious Blood of Jesus.* This book addresses some of the revelations concerning the areas that Jesus reviewed and revealed to me through the Word of God and by the Spirit of God during several visitations. I want to thank everyone who has encouraged me, assisted me, and prayed for me during the writing of this work. Special thanks to my wonderful wife, Kathi, for her love and dedication to the Lord and me. Thank you to a great staff for the wonderful job editing this book. Special thanks as well to all my friends who know about *The Precious Blood of Jesus* and how to operate in this for the next move of God's Spirit!

CONTENTS

INTRODUCTION

Unfolding the revelation of the Word of God brings about illumination of the authority of God. Today, it is vital that we understand that the demonic is entrenched in and is making headway into people's lives, but when you mention the blood and the name of Jesus, there is such an alarming reaction. The demons are very nervous about saying and teaching about the blood of Jesus.

If you want to see your ministry start to launch and if you are going to see the demonic pushed back, you need to talk about the blood. Speak out loud about it and thank God that you have an intercessor named Jesus Christ at the right hand of God, interceding for you; the perfect blood of Jesus has cleansed you from all your sins.

"Who is he who condemns? It is Christ who died, and furthermore is also risen, who is even at the right hand of God, who also makes intercession for us." (Romans 8:34)

CHAPTER ONE

Purchased by the Blood

*For God made Christ, who never sinned, to be
the offering for our sin, so that we could be
made right with God through Christ.*
—2 Corinthians 5:21 NLT

We need to understand that God has given us such incredible value. He desired us as a family and sent His only Son and purchased us. We now have a relationship with the Father and our great salvation by His work through the blood of Jesus. The provision has been made when we meet, drink the cup, eat the bread, and partake of the communion table—His covenant to us.

It is possible to walk with God here in synchronization with Heaven when we take care of the sin problem, take care of our position with God, and then take care of our relationship with God. As you synchronize your life with the life of the Spirit and with God, many problems that most people deal with go away because they are all resolved.

IN THE GARDEN

"I will put enmity between you and the woman, and between your seed and her Seed; He shall bruise your head, and you shall bruise His heel" (Genesis 3:15). In the garden, satan was told that his offspring would attack and bruise the heel of the offspring of Eve, the woman. The Messiah would come through the bloodline, and the serpent's offspring would be part of coming against that bloodline. This language was right there in Genesis in the first few chapters. The two most crucial weapons when dealing with the demonic are the name of Jesus and the blood of Jesus.

THE BLOOD OF JESUS

Demons don't like the blood of Jesus. Much of what happened with Jesus's ministry had to do with casting out demons, driving out devils, confronting the devil in the desert in the temptation, and dealing with how they reacted to Him. The blood is very powerful, and even the demons know it. Whenever I'm about to cast them out, they always say, "Don't mention the blood or the name of Jesus." Ever since the garden of Eden, it has been about the blood and genetics. The Levitical law prevents the drinking of blood because life is in the blood (Leviticus 17:14).

PERFECT SACRIFICE

Before He died, Jesus often hinted to the people about the process He would go through. And it's not like people were unfamiliar with sacrifice because, at that time, they were sacrificing animals. You have the spotless lamb, the Passover, and people understood that the lamb couldn't have any blemishes on it. This was because a blemish was a genetic flaw in the bloodline, so they had to be inspected.

When Jesus was talking about the fact that He was going to be handed over, crucified, die, and then be raised from the dead on the third day, He was telling them that He would be the sacrificial Lamb. But in the book of Revelation, we find that He was the Lamb slain from the world's foundation (Revelations 13:8). He was designated as the perfect sacrifice.

THE SEED

In the book of Genesis, Noah was perfect in his genetics. The eight people in the ark were qualified because they were perfect and had not interbred. In Genesis 6, God had to destroy the whole earth because of interbreeding. You can now understand that when you mention the blood of Jesus, it is what defeated the demonic. According to Scripture, the seed of satan and the seed of woman have been at war. So as in the days of Noah, we know that so shall it be before the coming of the Son of man. We know that there was some altering of genetics through the blood, which caused a nonhuman species, like a half-breed. And that blood was tainted because it wasn't pure human blood. Redemptively, Jesus came as a pure sacrifice, purely human.

It is important to God that you remain pure human stock. It is so valuable that satan wants to alter your DNA. God told the serpent, "I will put enmity between you and the woman, and between your seed and her Seed; He shall bruise your head, and you shall bruise His heel" (Genesis 3:15), revealing that satan has seed, which means he has children. Jesus confirmed this in John 8:44 when He spoke to the Pharisees and said, "You are of your father the devil, and the desires of your father you want to do." The devil, the serpent, has seed. A woman has children and seed but doesn't carry the seed; the man has the seed. Angels are never called sons of God; that is not what they are. The prophecy is talking about human offspring and satan's offspring.

The blood of Jesus is pure because He came as a human being of pure stock. All genetics are traced back through the lineages and reveal that no hybrid blood corrupted the line up to Mary. There was no interbreeding, and all those giant races were extinguished. Mankind can be dated back six thousand years on the Hebrew calendar and traced back through genealogies. It is all about the seed, the genetics, and the blood; they all work together. The Old Testament laws and everything that God told Moses to do had to do with the seed, the blood, and the generations. If someone sinned, the curse could carry onto the fourth generation (Exodus 34:7). However, with the technology coming forth, we can see where it is possible to alter your genetics. And so, you again get into similar events as those in the time of Noah, which is very critical.

We can see this play out in biology as well. If you were to take an introductory genetics class, you would quickly see what happens. When I was in school, our class conducted experiments; we used fruit flies because the traits from the different species could be easily identified. The flies had noticeable traits when you interbred them with each other. When they had babies, they grew up quickly and had more babies, so we could accelerate this process due to their short lifespan.

By the fourth generation, recessive genes are hidden but can still come out in offspring. If you take a married couple where both the husband and wife have specific characteristics (for instance, they both have black hair), a recessive gene will pop up in the fourth generation. If the recessive gene that comes from each parent is the perfect match, the baby will have red hair. You might think someone had been unfaithful, but it is just the nature of genetics.

WITHOUT SPOT OR BLEMISH

In the days of the law, the animal chosen for sacrifice had to be without blemish. It was genetically imperfect if a blemish showed up in the animal due to a genetic defect. You must remember that God made man and woman perfect at one point. Then the fall took place, and their eyes were opened. They ate the fruit and saw the difference between good and evil. They now knew the difference, whereas before they only knew good. There was no need for them to know evil.

God chose it to be that way because He is God. He can know evil and still choose good. His children, who are made in His image, couldn't because they were not God. They were made in the image of God; they were copies. They were second-generation and without the ability to make a good choice. If they were presented with evil, they could be seduced and deceived, whereas God could not. God can't be seduced or deceived.

Their disobedience resulted in an altered DNA in all the generations that followed. You can take their ages and look at the progressive decrease in life span down to 120 years old, which is where God said,

"You know what? I can't be with them. I can't strive with men anymore. I'm going to destroy them. Their years will be one hundred twenty, and that is it" (Genesis 6:3). Today, people live to be about eighty years old. However, they want to go to Heaven right now and don't want to live past seventy or eighty years old. Man's sin was so great that they were limited.

In Genesis 3:14–19, God was clear about the results of sin for man, woman, and the serpent. The serpent is satan; he used the form of a serpent. When God pronounced judgment on satan, He put him on his belly (Genesis 3:14). Judgment for disobedience pops up in every generation and goes down to the fourth generation.

Then, what about those who are obedient? Jesus, who is the spotless Lamb, was slain from the foundation of the world. In the Old Testament, the spotless lamb meant that the animal was without genetic defect. Therefore, Jesus was without genetic defect because He was pure human. It is all in genetics. He was a God-man, which is who Adam was. Adam was also a God-man, and he was made in the image of God. There was no difference when he stood beside God. To be "in the image of" means that you could put the image next to the original, and it will be tough to tell the difference.

God put the tree in the garden on purpose. He told them not to touch the tree because it was the only separation between God and man. He had to make a firewall. He had to make one thing to keep man and woman in check so they wouldn't think they were God.

THE NAME AND BLOOD OF JESUS

It can be difficult to think this way; we struggle with minor, everyday issues and can't even grasp the full impact of the fall. Imagine going to Heaven and seeing the original, seeing how it is supposed to be, and then being sent back. Imagine coming back and saying, "The Bible is true, and this is the way it is supposed to be, and Jesus bought us all back." When Jesus bought us back, He placed us with Him in the heavenly realms at the right hand of God and in the same authority (Ephesians 2). When we use His name, we have authority over serpents and scorpions, and we trample over them (Luke 10:19). We have power over all the enemy, over every disease.

The blood is so powerful, and the demons know it; it is so powerful in a human that, in most cases, a disease cannot attach itself unless there is a compromise in its defense system. The enemy must compromise the human body to gain access. The blood of Jesus is powerful because it cancels out the curse—it cancels out sin. The blood of Jesus takes it back to the day before anything happened. Everything was fine the day before the fall when Adam and Eve talked to God.

What we are dealing with today are the physical effects. The last enemy to be defeated is death because we still die. It is frustrating because it is true. The gospel, healing, prosperity, deliverance, and salvation are true. It is up to you and God to have a conversation about the blood. We are not seeing boldness because we are not sure what we are supposed to do. It all comes down to the blood; life is in the blood (Leviticus 17:14).

PRAYER

Father, we come before You, and we thank You for sending Your Son, Jesus, who destroyed the works of the enemy and broke the curse of sin through His blood. He destroyed the works of the flesh, and now we have the Spirit of God within us. You have restored us, and all sin is broken. Jesus, You reign, and we know that Your blood produces life in us. We don't have to fear because the blood covers us. In the blood, there is healing and everything we need to break curses off our lives.

You are restoring bodies and breaking generational curses as people read this. Lives are being healed, and You are releasing a boldness in Your people. You are releasing Your power in them and filling them to overflowing. They will go and proclaim the name of Jesus to others and set the captives free. They are being allowed to come in and know You. They are turning their lives over to You. We, as the church, will do the work of the Lord and not grow weary. We will have supernatural joy as we share You with others. We will tell of how You have opened the eyes of the blind and brought healing to the nations. We will see it in this day, and it is coming through Your people. We, the church, will be the ones to bring Your glorious light to a hopeless generation. We are Yours. We seek You in this day so that Your will is accomplished on earth as it is in Heaven. In the mighty name of Jesus. Amen.

What did the Holy Spirit reveal to you regarding this chapter?

_____

_____

_____

_____

_____

_____

_____

_____

_____

_____

_____

_____

_____

_____

_____

CHAPTER TWO

The High Priest Brings Good Things

*But Christ came as High Priest of the good
things to come, with the greater and more
perfect tabernacle not made with hands, that is,
not of this creation.*
—Hebrews 9:11

When Jesus entered the picture, He became the center of everything. Everyone looked forward to the cross until He came. Today, we look back at the cross. It is a circle, and everything is cyclical. You can see the center from God Himself on His throne from any position. God does not operate on a timeline, and if you see it as such, you can be deceived. He doesn't go by our calendar.

If you want to figure out God, you will have to know Him by His personality, revealed in His Word. Don't try to predict anything. Our predictions based on the Mayan calendar didn't work out, nor did Y2K, but there is one certain and historical event—Jesus died on the cross. God preplanned this central theme.

Hebrews 9:11 says that Christ came as the High Priest of the good things to come, so we can expect good things. It wasn't just the event of His coming; it was the result.

"Not with the blood of goats and calves, but with His own blood He entered the Most Holy Place once for all, having obtained eternal redemption. For if the blood of bulls and goats and the ashes of a heifer, sprinkling the unclean, sanctifies for the purifying of the flesh, how much more shall the blood of Christ, who through the eternal Spirit offered Himself without spot to God, cleanse your conscience from dead works to serve the living God?" (Hebrews 9:12–14)

The demons hate it when you talk about the blood of Jesus. Not only was that blood absolute, precious, and perfect for redemption, but then Jesus Himself became our High Priest. So not only did he give his blood and take our place, but then He is the one that delivered it and the one who represents us. Because of this book, I want you to be more aggressive against the enemy, who is trying to extinguish the human race, trying to kill, steal, and destroy and get into the bloodlines to taint people so that they are not fully human.

The High Priest, Jesus, is not going into a building or a temple. He is going into Heaven, presenting His blood, and speaking on our behalf. We know that Jesus' blood has a voice, and it is speaking. Jesus paid it all for us, and He entered the Holy Place, obtaining eternal redemption. "Eternal redemption" means that what He did is permanent through the Spirit.

Hebrews 4:14 tells us that we have a great High Priest in the Heavens: Jesus, the Son of God. We can cling to Him and trust in Him as Savior. Jesus understands our weakness and what it is to be human because He is now the One at the throne who is part human.

Jesus came in the flesh, and He still has His fleshly body. He has risen and is on the throne, representing us as a person who is both human and God. Jesus is

17

the God-man, so He can surely understand the human part of us because He was able to endure temptation; in His weaknesses, He stayed strong. He was tempted just like we are in every respect, yet never sinned

"Therefore let us [with privilege] with boldness approach the throne of grace [that is, the throne of God's gracious favor] with confidence and without fear, so that we can receive mercy [for our failures] and find [His amazing] grace to help in the time of need [an appropriate blessing coming just at the right moment] (Hebrews 4:16 AMP).

Hebrews 5 talks about the fact that the high priest was chosen on behalf of men, relating to the things of God that he may offer the gifts and sacrifices for sin. So he can deal gently with the spiritually ignorant and misguided since he is also subject to human weakness and is required to offer sacrifices for himself and the people because of his human weakness. One does not appropriate the honor of being a high priest for himself.

So now Christ came, and He didn't consider Himself as God. He became a servant and made Himself a High Priest, and God appointed Him to take our place as the intermediary. So right now, not only is Jesus the sacrifice, but He also has been able to sympathize as the high priest was human. And He offered up Himself, but now He is continually offering up His blood to the Father.

In his earthly life, Jesus offered up for Himself petitions and supplications, which were needed with fervent cries and tears to the one who could always save Him from death. And even though He was the Son of God, He was never disobedient, and He always submitted to the Father. He learned obedience through what He went through or what He suffered. Jesus was made perfect and prepared as the Savior. He is before the throne right now and seated at the right hand. He has offered up His blood, but He is also interceding with us and for us. When I was there with Him, He looked just as human as He does now, yet He looked like God.

The Scripture says that His sacrifice will cleanse your conscience. Your conscience is your soul, mind, will, and emotions. So essentially, Jesus is cleansing your soul from dead works. Dead works are manifestations of the flesh, and we deal with those every day. The blood of Jesus cleanses your conscience from the awareness of dead works. His blood reversed what happened when Adam and Eve ate from the tree in the garden.

SPIRITUAL WARFARE

You may think you have a devil problem, but the reality is the devil has a human problem. He can't do anything unless he gets you to do it for him. He tries to get the flesh to manifest. He can only do that by making you think you are the problem. He tries to come through your thoughts, but if you choose to concentrate on what Jesus did by cleansing your conscience from dead works to serve the living God, you don't have time for the enemy. Put him in his place and tell him, "Unless you want to pay for this, you need to leave right now because you don't have the things of God in mind. You have the things of man in mind." Cast him out.

"For the weapons of our warfare are not carnal but mighty in God for pulling down strongholds" (2 Corinthians 10:4). Spiritual warfare is bringing down every high thing that exalts itself above the knowledge of God and bringing into captivity every thought (2 Corinthians 10:5). Paul talks about spiritual warfare, but he flips it and talks about thoughts. Your thoughts are the battleground because satan knows that you are made in the image of God, and he is not. He must attempt to hijack you and get you to act. You have given him access if he can get you to agree with him. He had to get Eve to do it. It is all about choices. Where you are today is because of a choice you made yesterday. You say, "I don't know where this came from, and I don't know how this happened." Let's pull the tape; the enemy probably hijacked you.

A cherub told Eve that God was keeping something from her. He deceived her and said, "Don't you know that if you eat of this, you will be just like Him?" (Genesis 3:5). But we were like Him already, we were made in His image, and we didn't need to know what evil was (Genesis 1:26). That period was called The Age of Innocence. Fast forward to today, and you are redeemed. Your conscience is cleansed from dead works by the blood of Jesus to serve the living God. The enemy tries to remind you of your past and get you to commit the same sin again, but we know God is bigger.

"How much more, then, will the blood of Christ, who through the eternal Spirit offered himself unblemished to God, cleanse our consciences from acts that lead to death so that we may serve the living

God!" (Hebrews 9:14 NLT). The answer to all your problems is found in the above Scripture. At times, you may feel powerless, and you don't know why, but you are not powerless. The eternal Spirit caused Jesus to enforce this so that we would have freedom in our minds. He is all-powerful, and that is how much He cares for us and loves us. There will never be a point when God does not love you. God is love, and He will always love you, but if you want to be a friend of God, you will have to walk with Him as Adam and Eve did. They were friends of God. Enoch walked with God, and he was a friend. Moses was a friend, and he talked with God face to face. David was a friend of God, and the Bible refers to many others as friends of God.

IN HIS IMAGE

When God made mankind in His image, He formed us out of Himself and out of the dirt. The earthly body is your earth suit that you need to live here, but it is not the real you. As soon as you separate yourself from the earth, your body deteriorates back to the dirt.

I have died three times (because I was working too hard), and the last two times, I could hear my blood stop. On those two occasions, Kathi commanded me to come back, and I could hear her calling me. Around that time, a dear friend of ours took me to dinner during an overnight shift at work, and in tears, they shared with me. "The next time this happens, you are not coming back because you don't want to be here, and if you don't correct this problem, we are going to lose you, and we need you here." I corrected it, and I've never had another problem since.

I have encountered perfection, and one of the hardest things is knowing what God wants for a person but not seeing it happen unless we win them over. The devil tries to shut people down so that they are so mad they won't even talk to you. They end up passing away early, but it could have been stopped if people talked to one another as the church without wrinkle. "That He might present her to Himself a glorious church, not having spot or wrinkle or any such thing, but that she should be holy and without blemish" (Ephesians 5:27).

If we could speak to the church and build each other up as though the gates of hell cannot prevail against us, circumstances would change within twenty-four hours. Unfortunately, this is not the case because of division; satan knows that if we agree on anything, we will receive it, and he knows it better than we do.

We need to realize that Jesus paid for all this, and His blood completely erased everything in your past that hinders you. It guarantees your future because the blood cleanses you from dead works so that you will serve the living God.

PRAYER

Lord, we come before You and thank You for the blood that cleanses us of all unrighteousness. You are the one true living God, and we encounter full life through You. We thank You for directing and leading us in this life. In You, we have the power we need to go through life. We lift our heads and walk upright in our God-given authority on earth to see Your mission fulfilled here.

We love You and all that You are doing through us. We can make a difference here in every area of our lives and the lives of others. We will not sit on the sidelines, but we will go and proclaim You to the people we meet along the way. The enemy has no foothold in our lives, and we take every thought captive and declare the truth. We disagree with his lies, and we speak only what You are saying, God. You are the One we listen to, and we abide by Your ways. We won't give in to the flesh; we live by the Spirit of God and walk in Your truth in all that we do. In Jesus's name. Amen.

What did the Holy Spirit reveal to you regarding this chapter?

_____

_____

_____

_____

_____

_____

_____

_____

_____

_____

_____

_____

_____

_____

_____

_____

_____

CHAPTER THREE

The Blood of Jesus Is Your Assurance

*And for this reason He is the Mediator of the new
covenant, by means of death, for the redemption of
the transgressions under the first covenant,
that those who are called may receive
the promise of the eternal inheritance.*
—Hebrews 9:15

We have an eternal inheritance, and that reality shakes the devil. There is little information about how to live, thrive, and experience a high quality of life here on earth, but mankind was made to own everything. As a result of our ownership, satan works day and night to acquire what is ours, and he is manipulative and tries to monopolize you.

You must remember that satan is after our DNA and does not want people to know about the blood and the fact they have been redeemed. You must concentrate on the blood and keep yourself genetically clean. We are human and were originally given the earth, but satan stole it from Adam and Eve. Triumphantly, Jesus Christ bought us back.

When pastors and churches become lukewarm and ineffective, then Jesus must show up and write a letter, as in the book of Revelation, to these seven pastors because He can't talk to them Himself. Sadly, people fall because they become influenced by money or an agenda.

I have a pilot friend who flew for Southwest and used to fly a Lockheed U-2 spy plane. One day, the higher-ups in the company came to talk to him and the other pilots about how they were getting a new type of engine in the airplane. The pilots asked, "Will this engine ever fail?"

Of course, the higher-ups said, "No, it will never fail."

My friend replied, "Well, even if it doesn't have oil?" He asked that question because the plane flew at such a high altitude that if an engine did fail, they would only have twenty minutes of battery left to control the plane, but it could take more than forty minutes to land the plane. My friend and the other pilots shot down everything the men said.

But the higher-ups insisted, "Well, it can't fail."

A pilot responded, "You are saying it cannot fail, yet it is okay if it does. You will be in your office drinking coffee while we must spend ten minutes with no electrical power, at which point we will have to bail because the airplane will be unflyable."

Eventually, the pilots took their concerns to the engine manufacturers to enforce a higher standard. The manufacturers hadn't tested the altitude levels that the pilots were expected to fly. They asked, "What if all the oil drained out of the engine? Then how do we manage the unthinkable?"

People don't know how they are supposed to live, but according to the book of Hebrews, the blood of Jesus is speaking. The blood is testifying, and it was and is perfect. Many people believe in God and claim that they are Christians; however, only a small percentage believe in the born-again experience. The question is, can they fit through the narrow way because Jesus said, "few find it"? (Matthew 7:14). It is not an easy way, but it is the only way. The Scriptures have always been there, but we don't use them until we need them.

Noah made it on the ark because he was perfect in his generation. Jesus became the perfect sacrifice because He was perfect in His generation. At the end of the age, we must be careful not to compromise.

COVENANT WITH THE LORD

Genesis 12 talks about Abraham and how he gave his life to the Lord and came into covenant with Him; chapter 13 says Abraham was very rich in cattle and livestock. Deuteronomy 28:8 says, "Whatever you put your hand to, will prosper." In the time of famine, Isaac sowed and reaped a hundred-fold within a year when there was no rain, and everybody around him watched it happen. (Genesis 26:12). All these scenarios allow you to see what you have access to— God wants you to prosper.

If you want a product or service that works well, you usually must pay more for it. If you want the best, you will have to pay for it, but satan has made poverty one of the pillars of the church. He has convinced you that if you are poor, then you are also holy. You don't become holy with that mentality; instead, you become "wholly" ineffective.

We want to live a long and prosperous life, but what does God say about how long we live? God said we would live 120 years, and He is not limiting you. The blood of Jesus has taken off all the limitations. Your position in Him is through the blood. You cannot deny that satan and all his demons are bothered about the blood. They know that if you claim the blood of Jesus, speak about the blood of Jesus, and call on the blood of Jesus, everything they could do to you is ineffective. Don't stop believing that you *are* going to be healed. You will start a business and build a home, but you must get to the point where you will persevere. Then, if the devil comes against you or puts sickness on you, you go and build two homes. Don't back off! The Word of God and His blood is your assurance.

Why do you think the enemy goes after leadership? It is because a leader affects the most people. He struck the shepherd, which was Jesus, and the sheep were scattered (Matthew 26:31). The demons go for the high-value targets. If you accept that you are a highly valued target, then it is only a matter of time before you are ruling and reigning, and that is why the body of Christ is being attacked so much. Satan knows if you get bold about who you are through the blood of Jesus, you are a threat. The devils will get unnerved, and they will let go.

My mission is to activate you. I want you to see that we are in a famine right now, and all you need to do is sow like Isaac (Genesis 26:1). If you sow, a miracle will happen for you. I'm not talking about money. God is changing the environment through the body of Christ, not just through one individual. Never in the Bible did anyone make history when everything was going well. The people who changed history triumphed in times of impossibility.

I have been to the end, and I saw that everything works out, but how many generations have backed off thinking, *This is it?* It started in Thessalonica in AD 60, and Paul said, "Jesus isn't coming back until these things happen. Go back to work. If you don't work, you don't eat" (2 Thessalonians 3:10). They had quit their jobs because they thought Jesus was coming back any day.

The devil isn't backing off because he can't win. He is so desperate, but you have everything going for you. Your body right now is fighting certain sicknesses or diseases, and you will find out when you get to Heaven that you had cancer or some other illness. But because you changed your diet, you changed your Word and put your foot down, and things reversed, and you never knew you had a disease. It is all about how you perceive situations. What you believe is what you are going to do. I can tell what you believe by what you do (James 2:18). Begin to rest on the assurance of the blood of Jesus, then act on that assurance. It is truth, and it is our guarantee.

PRAYER

Father God, we stand firm in who we are as the body of believers. We will not be shaken or moved by anything we see. We are the victorious ones who overcome. We will not back down. We will do whatever You ask of us, Lord. We will rise above what is happening here and change history. We will not acknowledge the enemy but will put him in his place. We stand firm as a body, united on Your Word, and we won't move from it. Thank You for Your boldness in us, Lord, to go and accomplish what You have written in our books. I surrender my mouth and body to You to be used for Your glory. Teach me Your ways and attributes. Show me who You will have me speak to today to make a difference here to share the gospel message. I am fully Yours, Lord, and I thank You for giving me life today. Amen.

What did the Holy Spirit reveal to you regarding this chapter?

_____

_____

_____

_____

_____

_____

_____

_____

_____

_____

_____

_____

_____

_____

_____

_____

_____

_____

CHAPTER FOUR

God's Masterpiece

*For we are God's masterpiece. He has created us
anew in Christ Jesus, so we can do the good things
he planned for us long ago.*
—Ephesians 2:10 NLT

*But now you have been united with Christ Jesus.
Once you were far away from God, but now you
have been brought near to him through the blood.*
—Ephesians 2:13 NLT

I n the New Testament, we have the power of the
blood of Jesus Christ working in us. The Spirit of
God does not want you to take another step without
acknowledging the power of the blood. I am not just
talking about your past sins, which you should never

consider again, but referring to your future. Your future should be nothing less than glory because your past and future are taken care of. In this life, we should be asking Him, "What do we do now?"

Since October 2016, when I was on a well-known television program, I have been going full force in public ministry. Every day, I ask, "What do we do now?" I saw in Heaven our past is gone, our future is secure, but our present is up for grabs. Realize that life is a shopping spree, and you must go for the high-value items. By discerning your value and time, go after the unlimited opportunities God is giving you, then take them. I have seen that people don't discern their value and don't know who they are. Why? The opportunity given to them is not discernible because of our fallen position.

Based on the blood of Jesus and redemption, we should be able to receive from God but also give Him a return on what He gave us. I am not trying to hide it in the soil by not doing anything with it. I know what happened to the guy in the Bible who hid his talent in the soil; he was rebuked (Matthew 25:14–30.). What did he say to his Lord? He said, "I feared you because I knew you were a hard person to work for." It doesn't sound like a father/son relationship. The problem is that the church doesn't know that they are sons and daughters. We have been redeemed and bought back.

We are here at the end of the age, and everyone is arguing about angels, baptism, speaking in tongues, prosperity versus poverty, and sickness versus health as if these were an option. If you are filled with the Spirit and understand that you are a child of God, you would never think like that. You would never believe that your loving Father would make you sick, ever. Jesus did good, correcting all that the devil was doing, feeding the poor, and not taking money or food from them.

I don't respond to these kinds of questions because it bothers me that they are being asked. How could an angel produce offspring because they have different types of bodies? Jesus said, "When you die, you will be like them, not given in marriage or married." You can do the math on what is going on there. There will not be any offspring because you will be like the angels. When I was in Heaven, there was no gender, and you were way above the earthly body. We were sons of God, and it didn't matter if you were Sally or John; you were a son of the living

God. There is neither male nor female, for you are all one in Christ Jesus. (Galatians 3:28).

FOCUS ON YOUR FUTURE

Focus on honoring God by recognizing who you are while on earth. While people are fighting against prosperity, I am believing for twenty thousand dollars to give scholarships to businesses. I will provide scholarships for kids so that they can solo in an airplane, and it won't cost them a dime. When they get their solo, if they want, they can go on and become a pilot for an airline or fly their jet. I am not taking no for an answer, but someone must believe. Isn't it possible to refuse to get a dreadful disease? Well, I choose it to be me.

Why wouldn't someone want to say, "I'm going to sow this year in famine and start a business and reap one hundredfold like Isaac did"? Your dream is not money. You get a glimpse of your future, and your dream is a seed that is your future. It is the substance of things hoped for; it is the evidence, or the title deed, of things not seen (Hebrews 11:1). The Word is the title deed of things not seen; it belongs to you.

On May 6, 2021, my wife and I filmed a first responders' segment at our studio. I bought a Warrior Jet from a man I had never met in between shows. We both lived in different states, so everything was done electronically. I signed the document and sent it back to him in between shows. I grabbed my wife's hand and said, "Let's believe for the next one because we must be able to provide transportation for ministers, and we will get to a place where we will need to go places. We will need more than one jet because we will help people."

What if I hadn't done that? We wouldn't have what we have now, and it is not over yet. Why? Because I caught a glimpse that it is not about the money or things; it is that He will give you a glimpse of your future. Your future is your value, and it has always been that way. Your value was set before you were born because you were in Christ. Read any of Paul's books; he talks about the mysteries of being in Christ. Even good works were predetermined before God made man (Ephesians 2:10). God predetermined good works that would be done in Christ, and that means if you choose Christ, you have this list of things that you can do here—it was already predetermined.

Paul talks about how he was chosen and called to be an apostle from birth, and that was God's will for his life. Yet he did terrible things to Christians until he was almost thirty years old. Tragically, he had Stephen killed. He didn't do God's will for many years; he fought against God to where Jesus had to say, "Why are you fighting against me? Why do you persecute me?" (Acts 9:4). Miraculously, he was stopped while on the road to Damascus. It is the same for us; we need to be stopped and transformed. We must come to know our value and potential in Christ. He wrote a book about you with all the wonderful plans He predetermined for you as a new creation in Christ.

PRAYER

Thank You, Lord, that my value is found in You. I am not my own; I am fully Yours. I am Your child, and I will uphold Your righteousness here. I will fulfill the plan of God in my life. You have a specific future designed for me, including bringing Heaven to earth. Thank You for purifying me and giving me life through Your blood. Thank You that my wholeness is found in You. Thank You that it is Your breath in me. Thank You that I can live and serve You every day of my life. We, the body of believers, can come together in fellowship and agree that You offer salvation to anyone who believes in Your Son, Jesus, and that we will not perish but have everlasting life. You are my rock and foundation. Lord, thank You for accepting and loving me and determining my identity. I was made in your image, and You fully know me. Amen.

What did the Holy Spirit reveal to you regarding this chapter?

_____

_____

_____

_____

_____

_____

_____

_____

_____

_____

_____

_____

_____

_____

_____

_____

_____

CHAPTER FIVE

Called You Friends

No longer do I call you servants, for a servant
does not know what his master is doing; but
I have called you friends, for all things that
I heard from My Father I have made known
to you.
—John 15:15

It is time for you to step into your calling, and it starts with a seed. God gives you a seed, and then He shows you a glimpse of who you always were and how you will end up. From there, He sits, and He is sitting right now. He knows your name, saying, "What are they going to do with what they just heard?" The important part is that you know your future is taken care of and your past is gone. If you can grasp this and get with God, what would have happened tomorrow will not happen. You went into another chapter that was already written about you. He is waiting to see if you will do something about it.

I met Jesus and stood before Him. Jesus will not coerce you to do anything. He wants you to come to Him because you love Him. He waits to see if you allow the Spirit of God to reveal the information where it becomes a revelation. It must become a revelation to become experiential. If not, it is just information. If someone hands you a pamphlet with a coupon for one hundred dollars, and you drop it or throw it away without even looking at it, you miss out. It was informational, yet in your mind, you thought, *This always happens*, so you threw it away. What if it were something valid? How do you know the information didn't pertain to you? How do you know that an angel didn't hand that to you?

God will always give you provision for your vision. Provision is predetermined before God gives you your vision, and the provisions are already there. There are plenty of resources on the earth; they are just in the wrong hands. You will notice that many people are doing fine, but they are not under a covenant. Interestingly, you can own a patent for the problem and a patent for the solution, and it comes from the same person. It happens all the time.

God did it too. He did the whole thing and wrapped it up in Christ before the foundation of the world. Then, He sent Christ not only to announce the will of God but to demonstrate it. Interestingly, religious people will keep things non-relational. Have you ever noticed that religion is just cold? The religious mindset says, "You are going to hell unless you read your Bible more." Well, that obviously doesn't get you to Heaven; look at the Pharisees. You have religion pushing you, but the Holy Spirit is leading you. God has always been truthful and has always set the example.

RELATIONSHIP AND PARTNERSHIP

Jesus came back not just to announce who He is but He gave us three and a half years of demonstration. His relationship was presented with the Father. He told them, "You should be glad I am going back to the Father because I will send another like me. He will be a friend just like me, and He will reveal to you the truth and lead you into the truth. He will remind you of things that I have said and show you the future, and because I go to the Father, not only will you do the works I do, but greater works than these" (John 14:12; 16:5–15). That is relationship and partnership, not religion, and not Old Testament law.

"No longer do I call you servants, for a servant does not know what his master is doing; but I have called you friends, for all things that I heard from My Father I have made known to you" (John 15:15). Friends know the business's deep, intimate secrets and dealings because they are family. Do you remember what Jesus said to His mom? He said, "I had to be about my Father's business" (Luke 2:49). Jesus was twelve years old and was already doing the Father's work. I imagine He was listening to the Pharisees, gathering all the information and fact-checking what they said with the Holy Spirit.

The blood of Jesus didn't only resolve the past and secure your future; it assured a relationship and brought sonship. No devil can stay in the area if you are a son or a daughter. I saw in Heaven that we are way above the things we argue about here. Before Jesus left, in John 17, He was talking to His Father in front of the people, and He essentially said, "Father, I know You always hear me. I am doing this for the benefit of those who are listening. I want You to reveal to them and include them in the same unity You and I shared before the universes were lit up. You love them just as much as You love me. I want them to experience the same unity, love, and glory with Us." Jesus prayed for us, and He included all of us. We are all standing in that love, unity, and glory, but if we are still here tomorrow, what should we do? We do what Jesus said to do—the greater works!

PRAYER

Father, thank You that You gave us Jesus as the One we can call friend. We are never alone because You are always with us. Thank You that Your love is enough. We are not limited by anything, and we can share with You in every part of our lives. We can talk to You, and You know what we will say before we ever say it. We get to pray about everything, and we will see what we believe come to pass in Your name, Jesus. We won't fear because we are in You, and we are covered under Your shadow. You are the One we can run into for safety. You are always in our midst, and we are never alone. Amen.

What did the Holy Spirit reveal to you regarding this chapter?

_____

_____

_____

_____

_____

_____

_____

_____

_____

_____

_____

_____

_____

_____

_____

_____

_____

_____

CHAPTER SIX

Your Value Is Predetermined

*And Jesse made seven of his sons pass before Samuel.
And Samuel said to Jesse, "The Lord has not chosen
these." Then Samuel said to Jesse, "Are all your sons
here?" And he said, "There remains yet the youngest,
but behold, he is keeping the sheep." And Samuel said to
Jesse, "Send and get him, for we will not sit down till he
comes here." And he sent and brought him in. Now he
was ruddy and had beautiful eyes and was handsome.
And the Lord said, "Arise, anoint him, for this is he."
Then Samuel took the horn of oil and anointed him in the
midst of his brothers. And the Spirit of the Lord
rushed upon David from that day forward.
And Samuel rose up and went to Ramah.*
—1 Samuel 16:10–13 ESV

Y our value was predetermined by the Lord. I want you to remember this by first embarrassing *helel*, satan, who became the adversary. His value was set until sin took over. His name is helel, and if you read Isaiah 14:12 in Hebrew, you will see he is called helel.[1] The name lucifer was a Babylonian god. I don't know why the translators put that there because lucifer is not that Hebrew word. In Hebrew, helel translates to "bright and shining one of God." The name helel has God's name in it, *El*; the name lucifer does not. Micha*el*, Isra*el*, and Gabri*el* all have God's name in them. Ezekiel 28:12 says, referring to helel, "You were perfect, the sum or the seal of perfection," which means, "You received first place. Number one; the seal on the top of your head" or "the number one— the epitome of perfection" until iniquity was found in you. "Iniquity" in Hebrew is *'evel*, and its root is *'ăval,* which means "to twist, or distort,"[2] which satan did. He took the truth and twisted it.

---

[1] *Strong's Hebrew Lexicon (KJV)*, "H1966 – hêlēl," Blue Letter Bible.com, February 10, 2022, https://www.blueletterbible.org/lexicon/h1966/kjv/wlc/0-1.
[2] *Strong's Hebrew Lexicon (KJV)*, "H5765 - 'āval," Blue Letter Bible.com, February 10, 2022, https://www.blueletterbible.org/lexicon/h5765/kjv/wlc/0-1.

Ezekiel 28:12 is saying that helel's value was set until iniquity was found in him. He fell, and there is no redemption for angels or half-breeds. If helel was the epitome of perfection, how do you think it looked to him when Adam and Eve showed up in the garden, and they looked like God?

The cherubim, helel, was over the garden and was the marshal, the ambassador, and deputy over Eden. When he saw Adam and Eve, he didn't look like them, but when he saw God, they looked like Him. Adam and Eve were given dominion over everything, and God came down to walk with them, but he was not invited, so he felt left out and became twisted. Their relationship with God kept everything going, and he wanted to sabotage it by getting them to sin. We know that as a Christian, sin hurts your relationship and fellowship with God.

"My dear children, I am writing this to you so that you will not sin. But if anyone does sin, we have an advocate who pleads our case before the Father. He is Jesus Christ, the One who is truly righteous" (1 John 1:2 NLT). This Scripture says that we are not to sin as Christians, but if we do, it offers a solution. It says "if" because it is uncommon for a Christian to sin. But if we do, we have an Advocate, Jesus Christ, who pleads our case before the Father. If 1 John were taught more, believers would live right, and no demon would ever harass them.

You see, helel was the seal of perfection, but Adam and Eve were made in the image of God. Why are you taking second place right now? When a demon talks to me, I say, "You are kidding me. Are you really talking to me?" The devil problem you have is that you don't discern your value. If you knew that you were royalty, you would turn to your assistant in the spirit and say, "Off with their heads. How dare they talk to me!" You would be saying this because you know you are royalty, and you wouldn't consider anything satan says to you. If you knew that you had already won and are here on the earth accumulating your rewards, then why wouldn't you go all out? Whether you live or die, you are in Christ, so if you are going to live, keep on swinging and speaking the Word of God. The enemy knows your value; he doesn't want *you* to understand your value.

David knew his value, but his family didn't support him. He considered all this out in the pasture while tending sheep, having target practice, and playing his harp. He was out there, protecting his sheep and killing lions and bears. He must have thought, *Why did that man come out and pour oil over my head and say that I would be the next king when there is already a king, and I am a child?* He must have pondered this in his heart. David waited seventeen years to become king, and when he was sent to the battlefield to give food to his brothers, they were sitting in their tents doing nothing. King Saul was there, and he wasn't doing anything either, even though he was much taller and bigger than everyone else. You would think he would have handled Goliath and the Philistines. A natural leader would have gone out and done something about the enemy. David was the one to do it because he had discerned his value. He had been doing what he was supposed to be doing, and the situation and environment he had been in didn't taint him.

God honored him, and the anointing oil began working in David. In 1 Samuel 17:26, David walked in there and said, "Who is this uncircumcised Philistine, that he should defy the armies of the living God?" He asked that question because circumcision was a sign of the covenant. David knew the legal transaction had taken place and knew Israel's position because of the covenant. He was bold even as a child because he knew himself and understood history and the covenant. When David first arrived on the scene, Saul questioned his abilities as a warrior, but David explained that he used to tend sheep and had been prepared. David hadn't even left the job yet, but he discerned that this was his entrance. He had passed his test in preparation, and his opportunity was now. After David defeated Goliath, King Saul asked who David's father was. "What line did he come from, and who is his Father?" Why would he want to know that? It had to do with lineage, seed, and covenant.

Be assured that your entrance is now. I am not saying that to build you up emotionally, and I am not speaking from the soul. Realize that your entrance is now. The Lord is willing right now. He says, "I'm willing, but the flesh is weak." Every day, many opportunities are being passed up. When Jesus speaks and gives a word, He lets people take it, but they need to mix it with faith. Faith requires action, and that action destroys unbelief.

AGREEMENT WITH TRUTH

The action and agreement with truth are your remedies for unbelief. First is hearing the Word; then, it anchors you on a track that puts you in the right direction when you react and respond. If you could see the books that God has written about you, you would see that God has already given you the provision for what He wants to walk you into. If you go one step further in faith, agree with Him, and follow through, you will see the return. The Lord will show you the return on it because you took the Word, mixed it with faith, and put it into action. If you do not take the next step, you will need to wait until you get to Heaven to see what would have happened as a result of acting in faith.

PRAYER

Father God, thank You I have authority over the enemy's plans because I am in You and walk in victory. Jesus paid the price and destroyed the works of satan and the sin issue. I am free and no longer a slave to sin. I walk in the righteousness of God. I am fully loved and accepted by You. I am a child of God.

You, Lord, have given me power over all darkness, and I will stand in the authority I have in You over the enemy's lies. I remain yielded to You, Holy Spirit, and I purpose to respond by the Spirit in my life. Thank you for giving me boldness and strength in these days we are living. My faith and trust are in You. Today, when I go into the marketplace, give me the boldness to share Your goodness with others. In Jesus's mighty name. Amen.

What did the Holy Spirit reveal to you regarding this chapter?

_____

_____

_____

_____

_____

_____

_____

_____

_____

_____

_____

_____

_____

_____

_____

_____

_____

_____

_____

_____

DR. KEVIN L. ZADAI

CHAPTER SEVEN

The Spirit Wants to Take You Further

And though I bestow all my goods to feed the poor,
and though I give my body to be burned, but have
not love, it profits me nothing.
—1 Corinthians 13:3

Y ou can give everything to the poor, but if you don't have love, it is nothing. Notice that it doesn't say, "If you don't have faith." No, it says, "If you don't have love." You can replace the word *love* with *God* because God is love. I have faith because I have God, but it is based on a relationship with Him. Second Peter 1:4 says, "We are partakers of the divine nature"; we are in a partnership with Him. He had something already planned for us that was written before we were born. "Your eyes saw my substance, being yet unformed. And in Your book they all were written, The days fashioned for me, When as yet there were none of them" (Psalm 139:16).

There are no blank pages in our books; we will never get to some pages because of who God is. He is more than we could ever ask or imagine. Even if I wrote one hundred books, thousands more would be written in Heaven because God always does more. He provides for more than we could ask or think as though we will do it because that is how He thinks of you. Angels are the same way because they don't think you will ever turn them down, and they don't believe you will fail. They come to you with a word from God, and they want to deliver it and help you accomplish it. If you found out your best friend didn't believe in you, it shouldn't cause you to think less of yourself or think that God thinks anything different about you. What is written is more powerful than what people think or believe.

When I trained to be a lifeguard, most of the training was learning how not to be killed by those you are trying to rescue. I had to tread water with bricks in my hands as part of my test. It was bizarre. We had to tread water for seven minutes! I thought, *I can't even tread water with both my hands and feet. Now you are giving me bricks, and I can't even use my hands.* Another drill for part of the lifeguard training was that we had to swim up to the instructor, and he would put us in a headlock. Then he would hold us underwater for about a minute. The instructor won't let you up because that happens in a rescue when people need to live; you become a floating log. People are living in survival mode, and they are traumatized. They will have to hear from God on their own and keep going, no matter what. "For as many as are led by the Spirit of God, they are the sons of God" (Romans 8:14).

LED BY THE SPIRIT

Does it say that those who are led by prophets are the sons of God? No, it says, "Those who are led by the Spirit are sons of God." You are supposed to be hearing from God yourself. Prophets are supposed to speak and confirm what you have already heard from God. It has always been this way, so how did it get flipped?

An apostle is a "sent one." They are sent to a place to establish a work and ensure the doctrine is correct.

Their role is to help establish a local person to be the pastor, and then they move on. It was never about control or telling you who you could marry. If an apostle tells you who you will marry, even your dog won't listen. We are human, and we were not meant to be controlled.

I shouldn't be telling you something new. You should have heard for yourself and received the treasury of that knowledge, opened that vault, and known the secrets from God. Then, when a prophet comes along, they confirm what you have already heard. Prophets will always speak the truth, but it hardly ever comes to pass because people must mix it with faith. Jeremiah spoke it out, saying, "Israel, I have good plans for you. An expected end. Plans for you to prosper" (Jeremiah 29:11). What happened in AD 70? The temple was destroyed. The prophet Jeremiah spoke God's heart and said, "After four hundred years of captivity, I will lead you into the promised land." Now add forty years to that. What happened was not God's will. Those forty years were the people's will, and God let them have it.

We are going through things because the church let it happen—let's own it. God clearly showed what He wanted, and there was no other alternative. It is time for us to be changed. It will be just like Saul when he became Paul. He changed and became another man. Whenever people in the Bible encountered a prophet or the supernatural, it changed them. It was experiential; it wasn't just the Word, it was the experience, and there is a valid experience with Christ.

Jesus interprets what He says. He doesn't say something and then hope that you get it. The Spirit wants to take you further in what you have heard, but you will have to understand that the mode of operation of the enemy is to deceive you and keep you in a small place. He will cause you to wait for someone else, a kid, a David to come and challenge the enemy. I am focusing on the kids from now on because I know that I can get through to that generation and build them up.

I will not let this be handed off to a faithless or fatherless generation. That is the devil's mode, and that is why you should determine in your heart what you can do for this next generation and faithfully hand off the baton so they don't have to work extra hard and make up for what we didn't do. I want us to be known for discerning the time we lived in. We can't be the Monday-morning quarterback, sitting and criticizing what the quarterback should have done the day before. You have no idea what it's like unless you have been there. I was in a family with professional football players, and you can't sit there on Monday morning and say what you would have done when you can't even catch a pass thrown to you by any of them.

At times, I could not operate properly in the spirit realm because I was ignorant of what I was dealing with. Then, I would see men and women stand up and make the announcements, and the devils would vacate. I found out that it had nothing to do with what I thought; it was in what I knew. Smart people are quiet, they learn and then operate, and the manifestation happens.

PRAYER

Father, today I come before You and thank You that You are the One I can go to for everything in my life. Thank You that You love me, and You want to see me prosper in all that I do. You have called me a friend, and I can encounter Your presence. I trust You to lead my life and direct me. Thank You for taking me on a journey and bringing me through some of the most challenging moments. Take me further in all that You want to show me, Lord. I am fully surrendered to all that You have and want to do through my life. Thank you, Lord, for the joy set before me. Thank You for making all things new and that Your mercy is new every morning. In Jesus's name, Amen.

What did the Holy Spirit reveal to you regarding this chapter?

_____

_____

_____

_____

_____

_____

_____

_____

_____

_____

_____

_____

_____

_____

_____

_____

_____

_____

Relationship with the Father

He who dwells in the secret place of the Most High
shall abide under the shadow of the Almighty. I will
say of the Lord, "He is my refuge and my fortress;
My God, in Him I will trust."
—Psalm 91:1–2

You are full of authority, and you have been given the name of Jesus, the name above all names. What you don't realize is that the name of God is not pronounceable and not known. God spoke it to Moses, and he knew how to say it because he walked by Him in the cleft of the rock. He announced the name and was allowed to give it to Aaron, the high priest. Aaron was only allowed to announce it once a year, and it had to be with blood. He would go into the Holy of Holies and present the blood and the sacrifice, and once a year, he was allowed to say the name of God out loud (Hebrews 9:7). No one else knew it except those two. Then, when they transitioned to the next high priest, they were told.

After Jesus's death and resurrection, there is no more glory behind the curtain. It was Ichabod. In Hebrew, *kabod*[3] means "glory"; *Ichabod* means, "the glory has departed" (1 Samuel 4:21). Religious groups have been hiding that God left and there is no glory behind the curtain in the temple. Religion hides that God is not there. When the testing comes, we find out that God was not there.

It is all about a relationship with the Father, being known, and knowing how to operate. You know your name is known in Heaven, and it is written in the Lamb's book of life (Revelation 13:8).

When you stomp your foot on the *terra firma,* every demon knows that it wasn't a normal stomp because

---

[3] *Strong's Hebrew Lexicon (KJV)*, "H3519 - kāḇôḏ," Blue Letter Bible.com, February 11, 2022, https://www.blueletterbible.org/lexicon/h3519/kjv/wlc/0-1.

Jesus has given you the authority to trample on serpents and scorpions and given you power over all the enemy (Luke 10:19). When He said that, He was paraphrasing Psalm 91. He used the Old Testament because He was writing the New Testament, and He *was* the New Testament.

"A thousand may fall at your side, and ten thousand at your right hand; but it shall not come near you" (Psalm 91:7). Until we take our last breath, there will be crunching under our feet. There will always be thousands falling and ten thousand at your right hand, but it shall not come near you. It will always be true because it was already spoken. Regardless of what has happened in your or your family's life, it doesn't take away from the truth. Even if we are few, we are potent, and situations can change. All it takes is for one person to agree with Jesus.

People think that God knows everything, so they don't think they have to tell Him anything. If you think that, you are essentially saying, "If God knows everything, then why do I have to pray because God can do anything He wants. He is in control." You act as if it were all up to God and you were just waiting for Him, but that is so far from the truth.

God has done everything He is going to do. He is seated, and Jesus is sitting at the right hand. He is waiting for His enemies to become His footstool through the church. "From that time waiting till His enemies are made His footstool" (Hebrews 10:13). That means the church has been given the keys to the kingdom, and we are to bind and loose (Matthew 16:19).

"Now I say to you that you are Peter [which means *rock*], and upon this rock I will build my church, and all the powers of hell will not conquer it" (Matthew 16:18 NLT, definition added). Understand that Jesus was not talking about a brick-and-mortar building; if we as a church met outside, it would still be the church.

You are to give out of relationship because you want to. Paul said, "Don't give out of compulsion" (2 Corinthians 9:7). It is the same with praying. You pray because Jesus said you could ask whatever you desire, and it shall be done for you (John 14:13). Every day is a miracle because we have a relationship with Him. We are having this relationship with the Lord, and it is time we commit to Him and say, "Lord, I'm turning myself in because I need to go further, and I have reached my limit." Offer yourself to Him right now and receive His vision for your life. We must remember that He is the One who causes you to triumph and take dominion.

PRAYER

Father God, You are the majestic One, and we give You our highest praises. We worship You for Your mighty ways and acts, and we esteem You high and lifted up. Thank You that we have perfect health and that we are lacking nothing. Thank You for the gift of prophecy that is beginning to well up within. Thank You, Lord, that we as the church will not be silent but will speak of You and not grow weary. We are the victorious church You have placed in authority in the earth. We partake in what You have given to the church and uphold it in our lives. Thank You for interceding for us, Jesus. You are coming back to serve Your justice, and the earth will know You. We live to serve You all the days of our life. Thank You for giving us hope and strength today and in the days ahead. In Jesus's name. Amen.

What did the Holy Spirit reveal to you regarding this chapter?

_____

_____

_____

_____

_____

_____

_____

_____

_____

_____

_____

_____

_____

_____

_____

_____

_____

CHAPTER NINE

Angels on Assignment

For He shall give His angels charge over you, to keep you in all your ways. In their hands they shall bear you up, Lest you dash your foot against a stone.
—Psalm 91:11–12

Effectiveness in healing begins with yielding yourself to God. Everything we do is out of relationship with the Trinity, and it all starts with intimacy with Him. Operating in the gifts of the Spirit with the ministry of angels accompanying you begins with a relationship with Him, being sent on assignment, and walking in obedience. Angels are assigned to you to help you with this, but they can't operate if you are not yielded to the Father. These ministering spirits will help you when you are following the Spirit of God, you are not lazy, you are not in sin, and you are using the gifts of the Spirit. If you are on assignment or being sent and you are moving by the Spirit, the angels will accommodate you. They will go ahead of you to set up encounters so that you are led to certain people and speak to them.

Understand that angels don't witness to people—you do. Angels set it up, but you open your mouth and speak the gospel. I saw in Heaven that angels set you up, synchronizing with your books and what Heaven has for you, but you must agree with Heaven to walk in it. Your ministry begins when you are obedient; that obedience moves you onto a track, allowing the angels to come alongside you. Angels are just a cleanup crew for your mess if you are not on that track. The angel protects you and you walk away from it, but an angel's main purpose isn't to clean up your mess.

The Bible teaches that none of these things will come upon you, but if they do, the angels are there to lift you up so that you don't even stub your toe. The Aramaic says, "God sends angels with special orders to protect you wherever you go, defending you from all harm" (Psalm 91:11 TPT). The angels, God's special forces, are on special assignment to keep you in all your ways. The Lord wants to lead you into healing and into the healing of others.

Rest assured that the glory always works. Unfortunately, you may think that you need hands laid on you. I could pray for you, and you would feel what I'm walking in, but you are not walking in that. You are walking in what you are walking in. You will be changed by what I am walking in, but can you walk in what I walk in tomorrow when I am gone? If you want to walk in this, you will receive an impartation from being in the services, listening online, and hearing the Word. You hear it through the gifting in me, it is deposited into you, and you begin operating in it. There is a tangible impartation. It is not the written Word but the spoken Word. When you receive the impartation, you now walk in that yourself. You won't have to call for your angel because you are walking in it yourself. You will not be moved when you start to feel sick because you walk in the impartation.

In the past, anytime something bad happened, I would call someone to pray with me. Now, I can't remember the last time I asked for prayer. Tough situations happen every day, and I don't say, "Excuse me, let me call my prayer warrior." No, I take authority over it and don't react because demons can see that it is not working, so they go away. They go next door and bother somebody else.

You need angels around you all the time, and when they come, there is a difference. If you are walking in synchronization with the Spirit, you will have them around you. In other words, you must find out for yourself what you are supposed to be doing. You don't need a prophet to tell you that, but you need a prophet to confirm it.

Angels will accommodate you on your way because they are briefed on what should happen. There is a lot of discrepancy between what should be happening in your life and what is happening. It is time to clean things up and seal them up. Do not take unnecessary risks. Wait on God. When the angels come, you will feel as if you can do anything. I have found myself getting healed because the angels were present. They bring the throne room to you; they go back and forth to get energized and refreshed because many of you wear them out. The angels come and cause you to go further than you can go on your own. However, if you are in disobedience or lazy, another spirit will come, which you have allowed to be there.

You need to pray, build up your spirit in the Word of God, and have strong fellowship with people who are walking in this. Pray that God sends you someone, and when the angels come, stay in there with them. Do not get lazy, and do not believe every voice because many voices are out there. Your angels will cause you to move with the Spirit in greater measure because they carry that presence. Angels don't have healing; they have power, which causes you to get over yourself and receive miracles. If you begin to consider the visitation of angels and their help, they will back off because they don't want attention. They are better at glorifying God and giving Him credit than we are. They know not to touch the glory or to take any credit, purposely staying hidden. You don't see angels often, and they don't want your attention because they stay cloaked, but they want to help.

Have you ever noticed that you become overprotective and defensive when in survival mode or in an emergency? You may or may not want to admit it, but you are needy. The devil has you in that place, but God is not doing this to you. Somehow, you have found yourself in a pickle, and it is not all your fault. The Lord wants to walk you out of your mess, step by step. He wants to get you out of debt, and He wants to get you away from certain people. Angels want to help you with this. You must be careful not to push people away and isolate yourself. Your goal is to flip it on the enemy, get back on track, and begin to minister healing and freedom to others.

I have discovered that the only way people can control you is if you need them. If you don't need them, they can't control you. People become enslaved by satan because they feel they always need something. When these spirits get into churches, they cause churches and leadership to get into this control mode. For example, you might be anointed by God to prophesy, but when you prophesy, the power of God comes. The congregation sees that, and the pastor starts to feel as though he is going to lose the congregation because he doesn't have that gift. The body is supposed to be receiving prophecy, but if a person is needy or needs the attention to feel in control, then what happens is that you are no longer called on to prophesy.

Another example will be if people are being healed when you pray for them. Still, other congregants don't have that gift, so they begin to feel spiritually inadequate and worry about how others will view them. This boils down to an issue of control. We need to realize that being spiritual is about operating in whatever the Spirit of God has given you. You can't operate in everything because we all must have a turn and do our thing. The body needs to express itself and build each other up. People who feel the need to control are needy, and what they need is attention. They will dim your light because theirs needs to shine brighter.

When I came back from Heaven, I realized you must play by the established rules of the Spirit. We aren't bound to Moses's laws. The laws of the Spirit are to honor the way the Spirit of God and the angels operate. There is order, and it is all about obedience. We are not meant to question or argue with an angel, the Holy Spirit, or the Word of God. We are called to obedience.

Many of the struggles you encounter in your body are because you have been disobedient to the voice of God. Don't get stressed out about it; go back and repent. A lot of what you feel in your spirit is grief.

This is because the Holy Spirit doesn't have full access to you. You need to take certain steps, and if God has spoken clearly to you at one point, you need to go back to that place, sit with the Lord, and admit where you went wrong. He initially told you what to do, but you didn't heed it for some reason, and now you are here. You need to repent and return to the command He gave you. I had to do it, and I realized I didn't want to make any more missteps because now it would affect many people. I don't want to do something just because I had done it before and it worked. When you walk in the Spirit, you are submitted to your commander, so you must listen to Him.

If He has told you someone is not good for you and you disobey, you need to go to the Lord and ask, "What do I do now?" The problem is that many of us are entrapped because of relationships and commitments we have made with individuals. The Lord has allowed some of them to be there, and you chose to bring some of them into your life. It is time to go back to the Lord and reconcile. You must get that right so you can move forward. Once you do, the Spirit will start to walk you out of it, and your healing will come.

PRAYER

Father, we honor You and love You. We are Your warriors of the faith, and we hold tightly to the hope set before us. We know we will endure the trials but come out stronger. We thank You, Lord, that You are always with us, and You will never leave. We lean into You now and come to Your throne of grace. We are anchored in Your love, and we seek Your face today. In Jesus's name. Amen.

What did the Holy Spirit reveal to you regarding this chapter?

_____

_____

_____

_____

_____

_____

_____

_____

_____

_____

_____

_____

_____

_____

_____

_____

_____

CHAPTER TEN

Synchronizing with God

So in my sickness I say to you, "Lord, be my kind
healer. Heal my body and soul; heal me, God! For I
have confessed my sins to you."
—Psalm 41:4 TPT

You want to encounter angelic visitations, and you want the Lord to work with you and move you into synchronization, but men and women walk years before God and only days before men. Consider that it takes years of fellowship with God for mere days in ministry among men. Jesus's ministry was only three and a half years, and look what He did in that time, and we have much more than that.

In the church, everyone can come together in the Spirit. However, Paul would visit churches without leaving his jail cell. "You must call a meeting of the church. I will be present with you in spirit, and so will the power of our Lord Jesus" (1 Corinthians 5:4 NLT).

The apostle Paul and the Spirit of God were in unity with one another. We want to pursue this type of synchronization. The apostolic authority of Paul and the Spirit of God came together to address an issue in the church.

Similarly, Ananias and Sapphira should have just stayed home, but they showed up in church and lied to the Holy Spirit. Peter was there with the Holy Spirit, and he had to ask them why they lied; he said this by the Spirit. These are examples of synchronization, and coming together with God begins as a place of total surrender. If the Lord tells me not to give a prophetic word or lay hands on people, then I know there is a reason. If the Lord tells me not to visit churches and only rent convention centers, I say, "Yes, Sir." If He says, "Don't push for the offering. I will bring the money another way," then I just back off. I—and all of us—must trust God.

We have much to do for the kingdom, so we must avoid wasting time. You may need to stop associating with particular people and avoid listening to certain types of music and T.V. programming because it is poison. At some point you say, "I have given an hour to that, but now I have to give an hour to the Lord." Our time is precious and valuable to Him.

Professionals don't waste time, and they are always excelling. To excel at anything, you must do it two days a week to keep what you learned last week, but six days a week with one day off will make you a professional. You do not want to stand before Jesus and have the type of audit that I had. When I stood before the Lord, I had only done 35 percent of what I could have done, and I was a Rhema graduate. Kenneth Hagin laid hands on me twice, and I had the opportunity to sit under the best, along with well-known people prophesying over me. I had people who had done so much for me, but it was up to me to do something with what I had been given.

I didn't see Brother Hagin in Heaven, and Jesus didn't mention his name, but He talked about Moses, Lester Sumrall, and David. Everyone is a servant, and they want to talk to you. All the "big boys" are watching us right now and want to talk to you because you were chosen to wrap it up at the end of the age. They built the foundation and want to know what it is like to live in this time. You must do everything you can to stay alive, stay healthy, and make it possible for angels to direct you to people to witness to them and tell them that God loves them. You have been chosen to be a lethal threat to the enemy in this age.

RIGHT PLACE AT THE RIGHT TIME

Synchronization occurs because you are at the right place at the right time. You may have been hurt or gone through terrible things; however, you can still function in the accuracy of the Spirit. I am here to tell you that there is a pathway to your healing. Breaking the rejection cycle will take deliverance because spirits have attached themselves to your soul, which has caused you to be in a cycle of rejection. The demonic spirits have reinforced this rejection cycle, so you think that is who you are, but it is not.

You are supposed to receive your healing, and there is no reason you can't receive healing right now.

Angels bring you to the place to receive it, but they can't do it for you. Healing is received spiritually and comes from Heaven, making a transaction that manifests in your physical body.

God wants to walk you into your healing, but it takes getting right with Him. You may need to go back to a certain point in your life where something went wrong and repent and get it right. I don't attempt to find the person and apologize to them; I just repent and say, "Lord, I am sorry. Bless them and make it right." We all miss it sometimes, but we can get it right because the Lord is willing to forgive us. Allow Him to move in every part of you now so that you can be free.

Spend time with Him intimately and allow Him to speak to you. Be close to Him and know He loves you so very much. He has so many plans for you, and He wants to fulfill the books that He has written about you. You were made for such a time as this to be alive on the earth right now, and He wants to participate in that with you.

PRAYER

Father, we come to You with an open heart and pour our affection toward You. We ask for forgiveness for anything we have done that displeased You. Bring it up in our spirits now. We thank You that You are so gracious to forgive and remember it no more. We thank You for Your sovereignty and love. We move in whatever way You call us, and we are honored to do the work of the Lord in our ministries. We surrender it all right now, and we thank You for Your wisdom and direction in our lives to live it out with Your guidance. We give You all the praise. We worship You right now. Thank You for moving mightily in our lives in Jesus's name. Amen.

What did the Holy Spirit reveal to you regarding this chapter?

_____

_____

_____

_____

_____

_____

_____

_____

_____

_____

_____

_____

_____

_____

_____

_____

_____

_____

Salvation Prayer

Lord God,
I confess that I am a sinner.
I confess that I need Your Son, Jesus.
Please forgive me in His name.
Lord Jesus, I believe You died for me and that
You are alive and listening to me now.
I now turn from my sins and welcome You
into my heart. Come and take control of my life.
Make me the kind of person You want me to be.
Now, fill me with Your Holy Spirit, who will show
me how to live for You.
I acknowledge You before men
as my Savior and my Lord. In Jesus's name. Amen.

If you prayed this prayer, please contact us at
info@kevinzadai.com for more information and
materials.

We welcome you to join our network at
Warriornotes.tv for access to exclusive programming.

To enroll in our ministry school, go to:
www.Warriornotesschool.com.

**Visit www.KevinZadai.com for additional
ministry materials.**

About Dr. Kevin L. Zadai

Kevin Zadai, ThD, was called to the ministry at the age of ten. He attended Central Bible College in Springfield, Missouri, where he received a Bachelor of Arts in theology. Later, he received training in missions at Rhema Bible College and a ThD at Primus University. Dr. Kevin L. Zadai is dedicated to training Christians to live and operate in two realms at once—the supernatural and the natural.

At age thirty-one, Kevin met Jesus, got a second chance at life, and received a revelation that he could not fail because it's all rigged in our favor. Kevin holds a commercial pilot license and is retired from Southwest Airlines after twenty-nine years as a flight attendant. Kevin is the founder and president of Warrior Notes School of Ministry. He and his lovely wife, Kathi, reside in New Orleans, Louisiana.

Other Books and Study Guides
Dr. Kevin Zadai

Kevin has written over fifty books and study guides
Please see our website for a complete list of materials.
www.kevinzadai.com

60-Day Healing Devotional

60-Day Devotional: Encountering the Heavenly Sapphire

60-Day Devotional: The Holy Spirit

60-Day Devotional: Supernatural Finances

The Agenda of Angels

The Agenda of Angels: Study Guide

A Meeting Place with God, The Heavenly Encounters Series Volume 1

Days of Heaven on Earth

Days of Heaven on Earth: A Study Guide to the Days Ahead

Days of Heaven on Earth: Prayer and Confession Guide

Encountering God's Normal

Encountering God's Normal: Study Guide

Encountering God's Will

Encountering the Heavenly Sapphire: Study Guide

Warrior Notes Aviation
Volume 1: Flight
Manual Study Guide

Warrior Women
Volume 1: Study Guide

Warrior Women
Volume 2: Study Guide

Warrior Justice: A
Study Guide to
Experiencing Freedom
from
Demonic Oppression

You Can Hear God's
Voice

You Can Hear God's
Voice: Study Guide